SPIRIT OF APPALACHIAN KENTUCKY

A Photographic Journey

DEAN HILL

Keeping the "spirit" alive!

Dean Hill

Spirit of Appalachian Kentucky

Introduction

Appalachian Kentucky is a land of contrasts steeped in a rich history of exploration, cultural heritage, and in some instances, exploitation. Yet there is a connection, a closeness to this land that is almost impossible to explain, that keeps those that leave yearning for their homeland.

For those transplanted to the auto plants in Dayton, the steel mills of Indiana, or parts unknown, to be connected to Appalachian Kentucky is considered a privilege, and bragging rights are passed on from parent to offspring.

Visit my home and walk the ridges with me in spring. The dogwoods will be in bloom and maybe the mist will part allowing views of fertile valleys coming alive after a winter's rest.

Experience an afternoon thunderstorm rolling and echoing up the hollers as the summer rains churn up clouds of dust before sweeping across the thirsty landscapes.

Observe the autumn colors as they carelessly drift to the forest floor, no longer clinging to the trees after last night's frost loosens their dying grip. The lush carpet takes you back to childhood memories of mounds of leaves and endless dives and rolls and laughter.

Take in the pristine air of winter, invigorating and fresh, where the only sound is your breathing and the falling snow trickling through the tree branches.

Welcome to my home!

Spring

I tried to talk myself out of going to the top of the peak at Cumberland Gap. Rain came down in sheets throughout the night, and I did not relish the thought of a wasted trip.

Driving to the top I became less hopeful because of the heavy fog silently sweeping through the barren trees. I continued to question the weather and my sanity while I was walking to the overlook to set up my camera. I protected my equipment and myself as best as I could from the elements and waited...

The breeze picked up considerably. Patches of clear vistas appeared below. Suddenly the clouds parted and rolled along the ridges conforming to the rugged landscape before me.

I shot photographs for only a few minutes when the clouds took back the overlook. The brief peek of the valley was somehow meant to be I tell myself as I turn homeward. Persistence wins out!

As a youth I would climb the hills to the tops of the ridges only to look around. Turning in a full circle you can see endless rows of peaks and ridges in any direction.

Rusty barb wire fences which run along these ridges were being absorbed by the trees. These fences would converge on the knobs sometimes coming from three or four directions—designating ownership of a boundary of land. Fortunately one of these parcels was ours. A boundary to walk around, a place to explore...

The dark hollers come alive with colors in the spring. Ridges circle narrow hollers full of trillium, carpets of spring beauties, and many other flowers with names I do not know. Service berries are the first to light up the hill sides. Everywhere buds are ready to explode with all the colors and greenery of spring. To own a holler was to own the world!

Summer

Even on the mountain top it doesn't take long to feel the heat as the increasing light melts away the morning coolness. Dew soaks my pant legs while I move from location to location to determine the best position to photograph the panorama below.

Fog curls over the ridges and settles in the valleys allowing island peaks to rise up in a fantasy world. Clouds shimmer with motion in an ever changing scene. The sun peers over the far ridge—red and blazing. The carpet of fog begins to stir even faster. I do my job with the camera even as the sun reaches higher in the sky. The heat quickly melts away the mist... and then the magic is gone...

Summer is a growing time. You can practically hear the crops straining and expanding to fill any open space with rich greenery. Memories are of cool, foggy mornings followed by hot, humid afternoons creating booming thunderstorms that rock the hollers with thunder and blinding flashes of lightning.

This is a moment to sit back on the porch and retreat from the daily labors in the fields. A time to watch the waves of rain race along the hillsides of upturned leaves. I lean back on the porch, I close my eyes, and I allow the cooling breezes to coax me into a half–sleep/half–awake dream state... Thunderstorms pass through as quickly as they arrive, leaving a trail of dripping wetness. The trees continue raining down on the land long after the storm is passed. The sun pops out from behind the storm clouds running the temperature and the humidity up the scale.

My nap starts getting uncomfortable, and I know then it is time to move. Time to get back to work.

Autumn

It was getting late... The rain kept coming down, and we still had over two miles of hiking to reach our destination—Courthouse Rock in the Red River Gorge. This was trip number four, and the light still did not look promising.

We thought of turning back; yet, it felt good to hike after the long drive. Would the weather be kind to us? After all it had been raining for the past three days.

Upon arrival the weather gods were friendly and the rain slackened somewhat revealing a landscape wet and misty, rich in a tapestry of autumn's finest colors! Karen held the umbrella, and I feverishly worked the camera under the rapidly fading light...

Autumn is a time to reflect, a pause between seasons of two extremes—hot, humid summer days and the icy cold of winter.

The night skies are crystal clear filled with stars that go on forever or a harvest moon bright enough to read by. Frost fills the valleys with an icy reminder of what lies ahead.

Memories of harvests take me back to days gone–by of the family farm and barns full of burley tobacco curing in the breezes. Weather permitting we were okay until stripping. A cold, wet streak of weather meant fires in the barns to prevent rotting. A few times the whole family slept in the barns and attended these fires overnight. The garden was in its final stages. Vegetables were already canned or dried. The animals had their winter fur. A pile of coal was out back and ready. Being self–sufficient, we had to be prepared. There was no other way.

Winter

I grabbed my camera and sank into the forest floor becoming one with the rocks. The trees and I both braced for the onslaught. The deafening roar approached louder and louder as the fury nearly overwhelmed me.

Limbs shaking, snow blowing, and the unrelenting wind; treacherous and twisting, picking at every weakness. Sudden pockets of calmness... A moment to ease the tensions, the shivering... sighs of relief. What a day to be photographing the ridges. And the wind roared.

Another extreme of winter is the silence. An eerie calmness spreads over the landscape as a blanket of snow accumulates from snowflakes bouncing and slipping through barren branches. A silence broken only by shrills of laughter and yelling and hollering as we prepare for a fun day outdoors.

Too slick and cold for school but not to play! Our pony was geared up and tied to anything that would slide. Homemade sleds, a store–bought sleigh, a dishpan... There was no time to feel sorry for our steed. He would reap the rewards of an extra ear or two of corn at the end of the day.

A string of kids rode on the pony's back. Our homemade sleigh had runners waxed and loaded with the neighbor's kids; followed by the store–bought sleigh similarly loaded. Bringing up the rear was the dish pan with a single rider. Up and down the icy road we went. Add a kid here, leave one there. The infrequent traffic gave us wide berth and a knowing smile. For the day we owned the road, allowing only darkness to drive us inside to hot chocolate and a warm fire. ... and a deep sleep in a feather bed piled high with quilts.

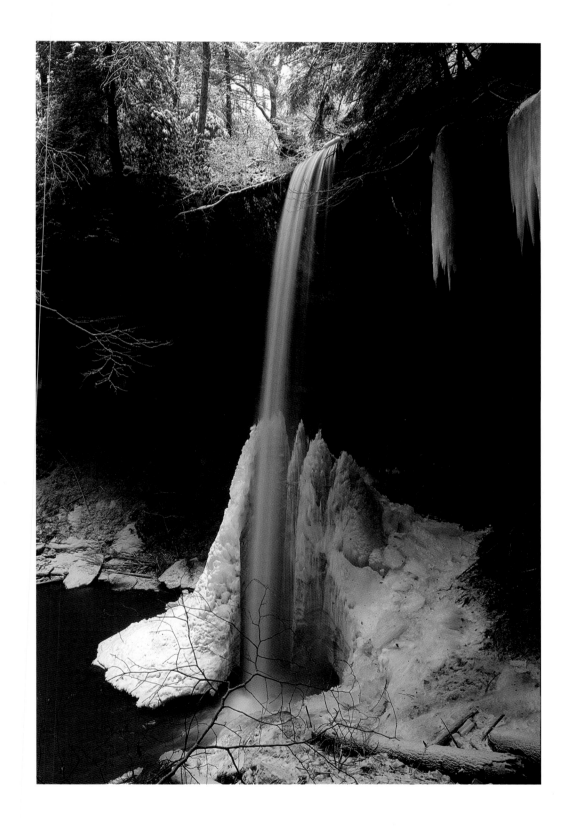

Epilogue

I attended an Appalachian Festival in Cincinnati this spring. We had a constant flow of people through our booth who were proud of their connection with "back home."

Viewing my photographs brought back fond memories of their Appalachian heritage. Many people took a few minutes to explain their roots. "I grew up near Hazard and remember everyone sitting on the porch talking and playing music in the evenings." "My brother and I helped our grandpa in the tobacco in Johnson County." Or, "I remember as a kid..." stories that I hear repeatedly throughout the region.

There were similar feelings that I took with me during my travels throughout many parts of the world. Feelings that were a reminder of a heritage so strong that the farther you got from it the closer you wanted to be.

Over the years I have come in full circle by returning home... A home up a holler in Appalachian Kentucky.

Index of Photographs

Winter

Acknowledgment

Trying to capture all the beauty of Appalachian Kentucky would most certainly fill volumes of books. Yet I had to draw a line somewhere in order to get this project to a printer.

Keeping focused was most difficult especially for an adventurous soul such as myself. Often times I wanted to go in two directions at once. Thanks to Leah Ben-david–Val and Sam Abell I was able to keep the book on course and flowing. Their advice and encouragement was invaluable to the completion of this project.

The design skills of Mim Adkins added to the excitement by giving me the first glimpse of what *Spirit of Appalachian Kentucky* would look like.

Thanks to Sam Mosley for his interest and knowledge on getting the book to print. Also, thanks to all the people I met during my travels throughout the region.

A special thanks to Karen for her patience, input, ideas, computer work, more patience, and tireless energy with the project. She always believed in me.

Lastly, I thank my parents for raising me on a farm in Appalachian Kentucky.

Published by Mortgage the Farm Publishing, 11607 Hwy 437 West Liberty, KY 41472

Designed by Dean and Karen Hill. Printed in Korea. First printing September 2004.

ISBN 0-9760616-0-0

Please visit www.deanhillphotography.com